Melinda and Bob,

You are two of earth's

best. "No one will take

your happiness from you!"

Thanks for everything.

Kathy & Terry

I CARE
ABOUT
YOUR
HAPPINESS

I CARE ABOUT YOUR HAPPINESS

QUOTATIONS FROM THE LOVE LETTERS
OF KAHLIL GIBRAN AND MARY HASKELL

Selected by Susan Polis Schutz
and Nancy Hoffman

Designed and Illustrated
by Dr. Stephen Schutz

Blue
Mountain
Arts inc.
Boulder, Colorado

© 1975 by Continental Publications

All rights reserved, including the right to reproduce this
book or portions thereof in any form.

Library of Congress Catalog Number: 75-39773
International Standard Book Number: 0-88396-015-X

Manufactured in the United States of America
Layout by Roger Ben Wilson

Blue Mountain Arts inc.
P.O. Box 4549   Boulder, Colorado 80302

First Printing: January, 1976
Second Printing: March, 1976

With permission from: Alfred Knopf, for use of quotations
and drawing on page 5 from Beloved Prophet. Edited by Virginia Hilu
© Copyright 1972 by Alfred Knopf.

Kahlil Gibran and Mary Haskell
drawn by Gibran

I care about your
happiness just as you
care about mine.
I could not be at peace
if you were not.

Kahlil Gibran from Mary Haskell's Journal
May 27, 1923

Nothing you become will
disappoint me; I have no precon-
ception that I'd like to see
you be or do. I have no desire to
foresee you, only to discover
you. You can't disappoint me.

Mary Haskell's letter
November 23, 1912

A man can be free
without being great, but
no man can be great
without being free.

Kahlil Gibran's letter
May 16, 1913

Sometimes you have
not even begun
to speak—and I am at
the end of what
you are saying.

Kahlil Gibran, from Mary Haskell's Journal
July 28, 1917

You have helped me in my work
and in myself. And I have
helped you in your work and in
yourself. And I am grateful
to heaven for this you-and-me.

Kahlil Gibran from Mary Haskell's Journal
March 12, 1922

The idea of God is
different in every man,
and one can never
give another his own
religion.

From Mary Haskell's Journal
September 14, 1920

Demonstrations of love
are small, compared
with the great thing that
is back of them.

Kahlil Gibran from Mary Haskell's Journal
April 28, 1922

... it's a test of a person—to
say hard things. Whenever
I've tested you you've just
been more ... And at these
times a strange sense
comes to me ... —a sense of
a faraway childhood
with you—very beautiful. I see
bright fields and you
and I are in them, together,
children.

Mary Haskell's Journal
June 11, 1912

What-To-Love is a
fundamental human problem.
And if we have this
solution—Love what may Be
—we see that this is
the way Reality loves—and
that there is no other
loving that lasts or
understands.

Mary Haskell's letter
February 2, 1915

I am so happy in your
happiness. To you happiness
is a form of freedom,
and of all the people I know
you should be the freest.
Surely you have earned this
happiness and this freedom.
Life cannot be but kind
and sweet to you. You have
been so sweet and kind
to life.

Kahlil Gibran's letter
January 24, 1923

When I am a stranger in a large
city I like to sleep in different
rooms, eat in different places,
walk through unknown
streets, and watch the unknown
people who pass. I love
to be the solitary traveler!

From Kahlil Gibran's letter
May 16, 1911

I want to do a great deal of
walking in the open country. Just
think, Mary, of being caught
by thunder storms! Is there
a sight more wonderful than that
of seeing the elements
producing life through pure
motion?

From Kahlil Gibran's letter
May 24, 1914

**Knowledge is Life
with wings.**

Kahlil Gibran's letter
November 15, 1917

People are always longing for
someone to help them realize
their best selves, to understand their
hidden self, to believe in them
and demand their best. When we can
do this for people, we ought
not to withhold it. We ought not to
be just an ear to them.

Mary Haskell's Journal
April 18, 1920, New York.

... what the soul knows
is often unknown to
the man who has a soul.
We are infinitely
more than we think.

Kahlil Gibran's letter
October 6, 1915

To think about oneself is terrifying.
But it is the only honest thing:
to think about myself as I am, my
ugly features, my beautiful features,
and wonder at them. What
other solid beginning can I have,
what to make progress from
except myself?

Mary Haskell's Journal
September 10, 1920

Marriage doesn't give one any
rights in another person
except such rights as that per-
son gives—nor any freedom
except the freedom which that
person gives.

Kahlil Gibran from Mary Haskell's Journal
May 27, 1923

Among intelligent people the
surest basis for marriage
is friendship—the sharing of
real interests—the ability
to fight out ideas together and
understand each other's
thoughts and dreams.

Kahlil Gibran from Mary Haskell's Journal
May 26, 1923

What difference does it
make, whether you
live in a big city or in a
community of homes?
The real life is within.

Kahlil Gibran from Mary Haskell's Journal
May 27, 1923

But now I put myself in your
hands. You can put
yourself in another person's
hands when he knows
what you are doing and has
respect for it and loves
it. He gives you
your freedom.

Mary Haskell's Journal
June 20, 1914

Mary, what is there in a storm that
moves me so? Why am I so much
better and stronger and more certain
of life while a storm is passing?
I do not know, and yet I love a storm
more, far more, than anything
in nature.

Kahlil Gibran's letter
August 14, 1912

I often picture myself living on
a mountain top, in the
most stormy country (not the
coldest) in the world.
Is there such a place? If there
is I shall go to it someday
and turn my heart into pictures
and poems.

Kahlil Gibran's letter
March 1, 1914

Imagination sees the complete reality,—
it is where past, present and future
meet—. . . Imagination is limited neither
to the reality which is apparent—
nor to one place. It lives everywhere. It
is at a centre and feels the vibrations
of all the circles within which east and
west are vitally included. Imagination
is the life of mental freedom. It
realizes what everything is in its many
aspects. —Imagination does not
uplift: we don't want to be uplifted, we
want to be more completely aware.

Kahlil Gibran, from Mary Haskell's Journal
June 7, 1912

We unconsciously contradict
ourselves when we say we
like a man's style and not his
ideas. Style and ideas
are one.

From Mary Haskell's Journal
June 2, 1912

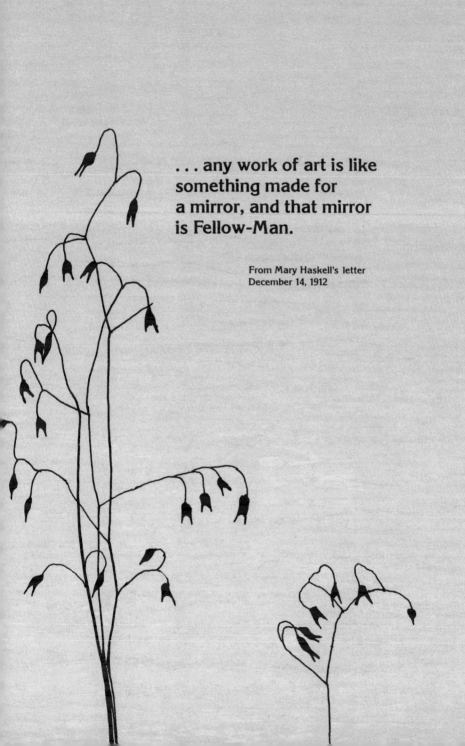

. . . any work of art is like
something made for
a mirror, and that mirror
is Fellow-Man.

From Mary Haskell's letter
December 14, 1912

What is poetry? "An
extension of vision—
and music is an
extension of hearing."

Kahlil Gibran from Mary Haskell's Journal
June 20, 1914

When the hand of Life is heavy
and night songless, it is
the time for love and trust. And
how light the hand of life
becomes and how songful the
night, when one is loving
and trusting all.

From Kahlil Gibran's letter
December 19, 1916

Isn't it better to desire and
to change and lift the
desire to something higher
—than not to desire?

Mary Haskell's Journal
April 17, 1911,

A true hermit goes to
the wilderness to
find not to lose himself.

Kahlil Gibran's letter
October 8, 1913

If I accept the sunshine
and warmth I must
also accept the thunder
and the lightning.

Kahlil Gibran from Mary Haskell's Journal
March 12, 1922,

I wish I could come in to you as my
mother used to come to me in the
many illnesses I used to have—and as
your mother must have come to
you—like Life when I was empty of life—
so freshly quiet and comforting,
like sweet cool water, because I knew
she loved me and bore me in her
thought, and I had no fear. Always a
peace was laid then upon my
restlessness. I drank something beyond
my craving from her presence, and
for the moments she stayed my memory
of suffering is as of a step by which
I mounted to a clearer joy in feeling her,
a more exquisite sense of her.

From Mary Haskell's letter
February 16, 1912

If I can open a new corner in a man's own heart to him I have not lived in vain. Life itself is the thing, not joy or pain or happiness or unhappiness. To hate is as good as to love—an enemy may be as good as a friend. Live for yourself —live your life. Then you are most truly the friend of man. —I am different every day—and when I am eighty, I shall still be experimenting and changing. Work that I have done no longer concerns me—it is past. I have too much on hand in life itself.

Kahlil Gibran, from Mary Haskell's Journal
December 25, 1912

I realized, that all the trouble I ever had about you came from some smallness or fear in myself.

From Mary Haskell's Journal
June 12, 1912

... follow your heart. Your heart is
the right guide in everything
big. Mine is so limited. What you
want to do is determined by
that divine element that is in each
of us.

Kahlil Gibran from Mary Haskell's Journal
March 12, 1922

Find out the best in a person and tell him
about it. We all need that. I have
grown up on praise—and it has made me
humble. It will always make a
person long to deserve the praise. And
any real consciousness is aware
of something much greater than itself.
Praise means understanding. We
all are fine and great, fundamentally;
overestimation of one another is
impossible. Learn to see the greatness
and the loveliness in one another—
—and to tell one another of it when
we see it.

Mary Haskell's Journal
January 14, 1922

The relation between you
and me is the most
beautiful thing in my life. It
is the most wonderful
thing that I have known in
any life. It is eternal.

Kahlil Gibran from Mary Haskell's Journal
September 11, 1922

... an expression of that sacred
desire to find this world and
to behold it naked; and that is the
soul of the poetry of Life.
Poets are not merely those who write
poetry, but those whose hearts
are full of the spirit of life.

Kahlil Gibran's letter
July 17, 1915

We need to learn to be our own critics. A
poet has a vision, when he is in
another world. He comes back from that
world and he tries to tell his vision.
He may not get the actual thing into his
poem at all, or, if he is an artist,
into his picture. But when he reads his
poem, every line in it reminds him
of something in his vision, and he lives
the vision over again as he reads.

Mary Haskell's Journal dated
September 7, 1920

The professors in the academy say, "Do not make the model more beautiful than she is,"and my soul whispers, "O if you could only paint the model as beautiful as she really is."

Kahlil Gibran's letter
November 8, 1908

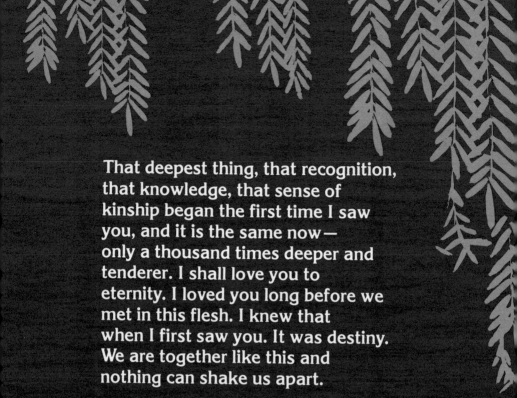

That deepest thing, that recognition,
that knowledge, that sense of
kinship began the first time I saw
you, and it is the same now—
only a thousand times deeper and
tenderer. I shall love you to
eternity. I loved you long before we
met in this flesh. I knew that
when I first saw you. It was destiny.
We are together like this and
nothing can shake us apart.

Kahlil Gibran from Mary Haskell's Journal
March 12, 1922

Each and every one of us, dear
Mary, must have a resting
place somewhere. The resting
place of my soul is a beautiful
grove where my knowledge
of you lives.

Kahlil Gibran's letter
November 8, 1908

51

We are expressions of earth
and of life—not separate
individuals only. We cannot
get enough away from
the earth to see the earth and
ourselves as separates.
We move with its great move-
ments and our growth
is part of its great growth.

Kahlil Gibran from Mary Haskell's Journal
May 5, 1922

The trees were budding, the
birds were singing—
the grass was wet—the
whole earth was shining.
And suddenly I was
the trees and the flowers
and the birds and
the grass—and there was no
I at all.

Kahlil Gibran from Mary Haskell's Journal
May 23, 1924

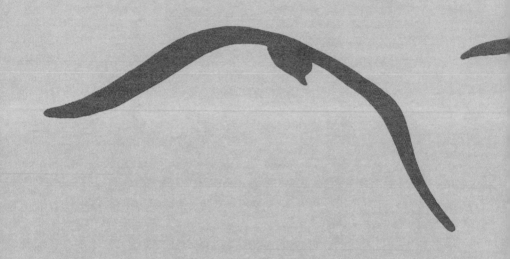

Let me, O let me bathe my soul
in colours; let me swallow the
sunset and drink the rainbow.

Kahlil Gibran's letter
November 8, 1908

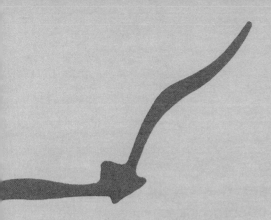

The most wonderful thing, Mary, is
that you and I are always walking
together, hand in hand, in a strangely
beautiful world, unknown to
other people. We both stretch one
hand to receive from Life—and
Life is generous indeed.

Kahlil Gibran's letter
October 22, 1912

When two people meet, they ought to be
like two water lilies opening side
by side, each showing its golden heart,
not closed up tight, and reflecting
the pond, the trees, and the sky. And
there is too much of the closed
heart. When I come to you, we talk for
four or six hours. If I'm going to
take six hours of your time, I ought to
unfold for you, and to be sure that
it is myself I give.

Mary Haskell's Journal
September 10, 1920

"With you, Mary," he said today, "I want to be just like a blade of grass, that moves as the air moves it— to talk just according to the impulse of the moment. And I do."

Kahlil Gibran, from Mary Haskell's Journal
January 10, 1914

His love is as restful as Nature
itself. He has no standard
for you to conform to, no choice
about you, but is simply
with your reality, just as Nature
is. You are real, so is he:
the two realities love each other
—voilà!

From Mary Haskell's Journal
December 29, 1912

No human relation gives
one possession in another—
every two souls are
absolutely different. In
friendship or in love, the two
side by side raise hands
together to find what one
cannot reach alone.

Kahlil Gibran from Mary Haskell's Journal
June 8, 1924,

I want to be alive
to all the life that is in
me now, to know
each moment to the
uttermost.

Kahlil Gibran, from Mary Haskell's Journal
June 7, 1912

You listen to so much
more than I can say.
You hear conscious-
ness. You go with me
where the words
I say can't carry you.

Kahlil Gibran from Mary Haskell's Journal
June 5, 1924